ILLUSTRATED DICTIONARY OF PHYSICAL GEOGRAPHY

Henry T. Conserva
Illustrated by:
Albert Petrik

PREFACE

This *Illustrated Dictionary of Physical Geography* is the result of my reactions to problems I faced teaching geography in public secondary schools in an urban environment. I was never surprised by the fact that geographical knowledge among my students was minimal for this condition seems to be a nationwide phenomenon. More to the point, students seemed to have difficulty understanding many geographical concepts without some visual aids to learning. I found that if I illustrated a geographical term on the blackboard, students could more easily comprehend it. This seemed to be true of all my students from the native born to the "newcomer." The story doesn't end here. In my researching geographical terms, I found vagueness and confusion in the vocabulary of this subject. The Caspian Sea is really a salt lake. One region's hill is another's mountain and a creek in some places would seem like a river to visitors from arid places. Confusion notwithstanding, geography teachers need all the help that they can get in building the students' vocabulary and I hope that this dictionary will be of good use.

I have italicized the defined words found in this dictionary for easy cross reference.

Henry T. Conserva
Sonoma, California

ABYSSAL PLAIN

A large, flat area of the *ocean* floor

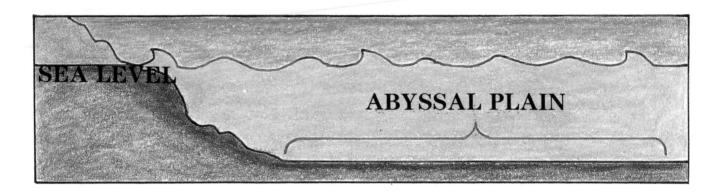

ALLUVIAL FAN

a fan-shaped accumulation of alluvium deposited at the mouth of
a ravine....alluvium is any sediment deposited by flowing water
....a ravine is a deep *gorge* in the *earth's* surface worn by the
flow of water.

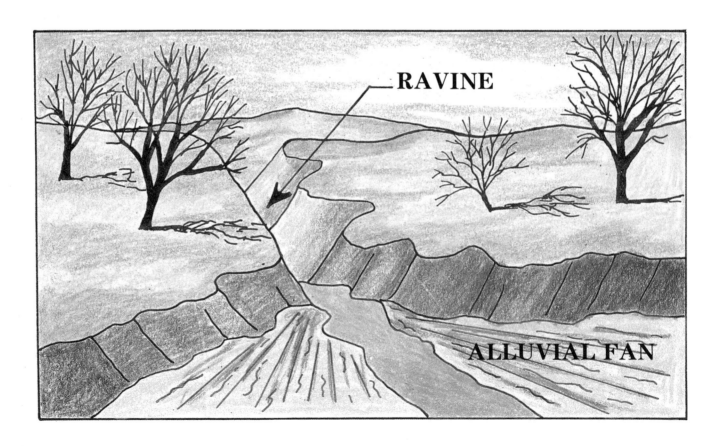

ANTARCTIC CIRCLE

The *parallel* of *latitude* drawn at 66-½° south of the *Equator*

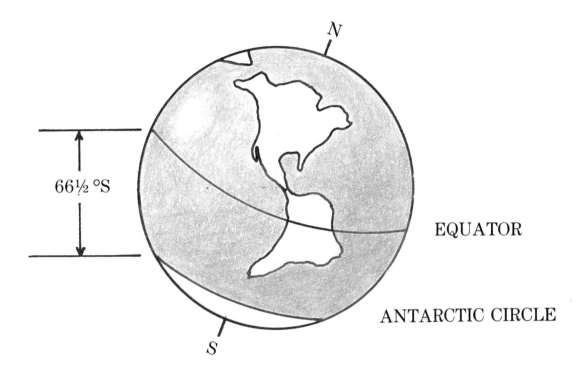

66½ °S

N

EQUATOR

ANTARCTIC CIRCLE

S

AQUIFER

A water bearing rock formation

(underground layer of rock bearing water
which can rise to the surface through cracks
in the earth to form wells, lakes, and
other water forms.)

ARCHIPELAGO

A group of *islands*

ARCTIC CIRCLE

The *parallel* of *latitude* drawn at 66-½° north of the *Equator*

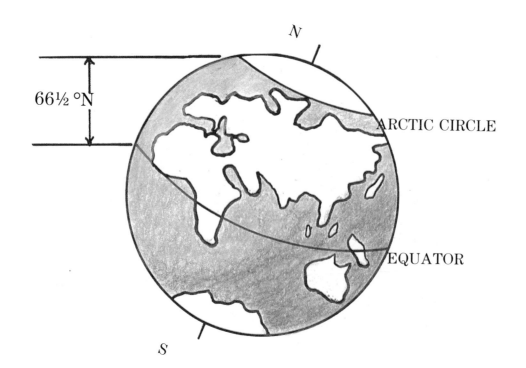

ARTESIAN WELL

A well which gives a continuous flow of water forced upwards
by pressure due to the outlet of the well being below the level
of the source of the water.

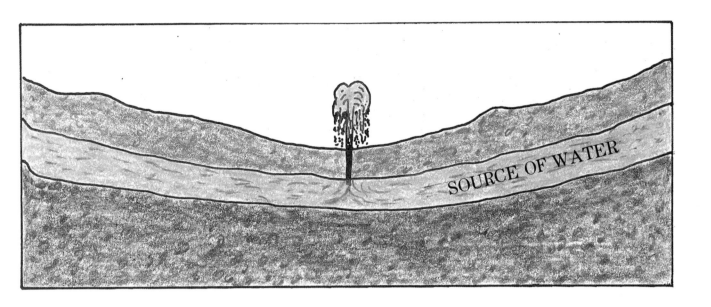

SOURCE OF WATER

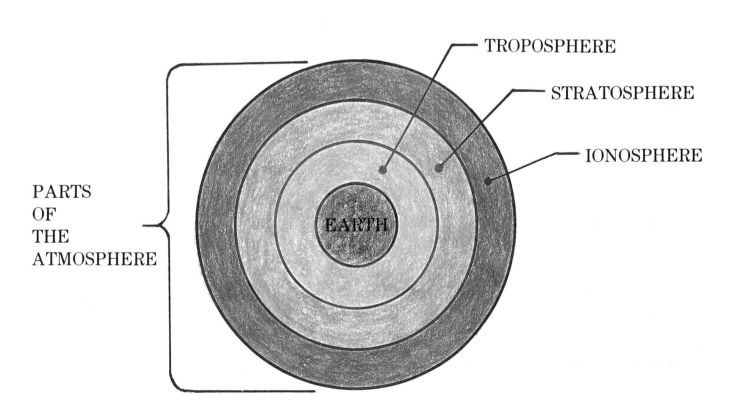

PARTS
OF
THE
ATMOSPHERE

EARTH

TROPOSPHERE

STRATOSPHERE

IONOSPHERE

ATOLL

A coral *reef* in the shape of a ring or horseshoe enclosing a
lagoon

LAGOON

AVALANCHE

A vast mass of snow and ice at high altitude which has accumulated
to such an extent that its own weight causes it to slide rapidly
down the *mountain* slope, often carrying with it thousands of tons
of rock

AXIS

The imaginary line, joining the *North Pole* and the *South Pole* through the center of the *earth*, on which the *earth* rotates once every twenty four hours. It has a fixed inclination of 66-½ ° to the plane of the *earth's* orbit.

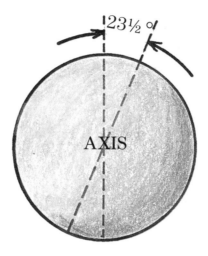

BADLANDS

An area of barren land characterized by roughly eroded ridges, *peaks*, and *mesas*

BANK

The sloping ground along the edge of a *river, stream,* or *lake*

BAR

A ridge of sand and rock fragments formed across the mouth of
a *river* or the entrance to a *bay*

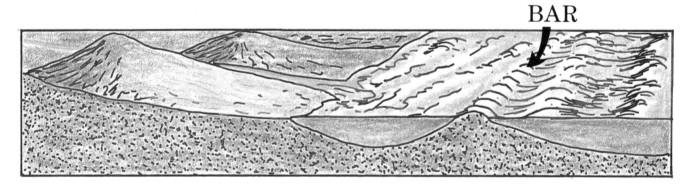

BASIN

The land drained by a *river;* any depression in the *Earth's* surface

BAY

A wide indentation into the land, formed by the *sea* or a *lake*

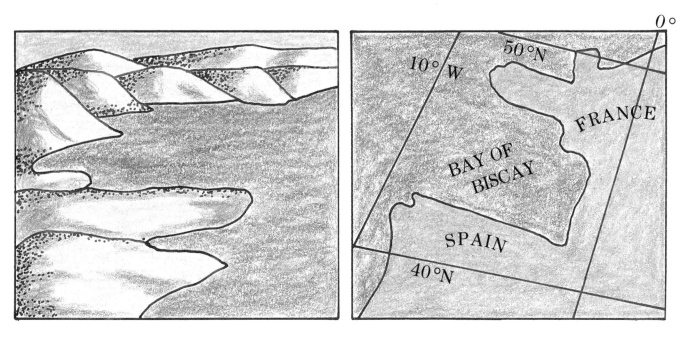

BAYOU

A marshy, sluggish body of water *tributary* to a *river*

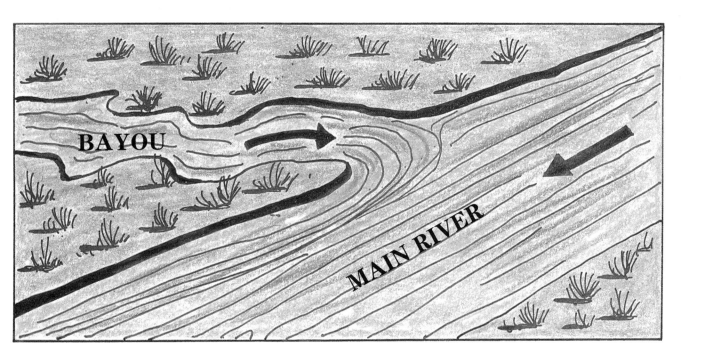

BEACH

The land along the edge of an *ocean, sea, lake,* or *river,*
especially when sandy or pebbly

BIGHT

An indentation in the seacoast larger or with a gentler curvature than a
bay

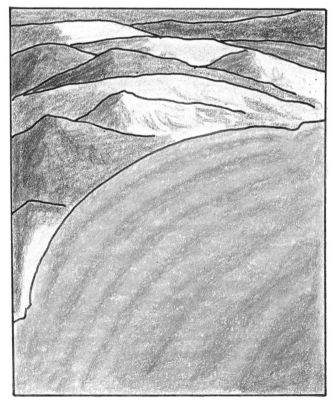

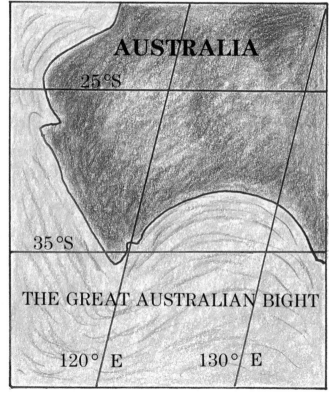

BLUFF

A *cliff* with an almost perpendicular front often found by a *river*.

BUTTE

An isolated *hill*

CALDERA

A large *basin*-shaped crater surrounded by steep *cliffs*, often formed by the collapse of the top of a volcanic *mountain*.

CANYON

A *gorge* of considerable size, narrow, and bounded by steep slopes.

CAPE

A pointed piece of land jutting out into the *sea*

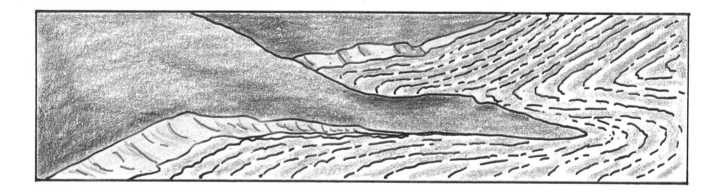

CARDINAL POINTS

The four main directions or points of the compass: North, South
East, and West

CATARACT

A great *waterfall,* or a series of falls

CAVE

A natural underground
chamber open to the surface

CAVERN

A large, roofed-over, cavity in any kind of rock

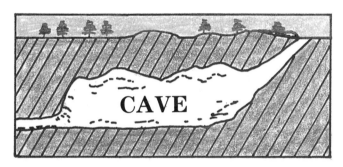

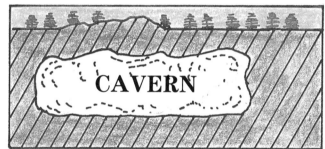

CHANNEL

A narrow stretch of *sea* between two land masses, and connecting two more
extensive areas of *sea.* A broad *strait.*

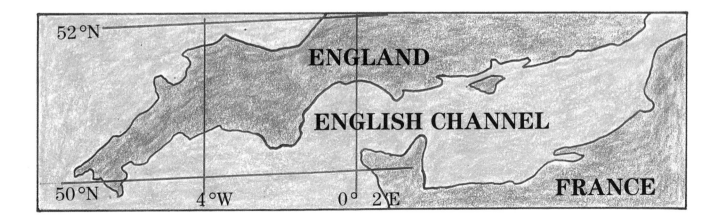

CINDER CONE

The conical *hill* built up with the ejected material from a *volcano*

CINDER CONE

CLIFF

A high steep rock face

CLIMATE

The average weather conditions of a place or region throughout the *season*.

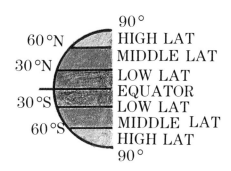

BASIC CLIMATE CHART

I. LOW LATITUDE TROPICAL CLIMATES (0° to 30°)

A. RAINFOREST: High temperature all during the year with great amounts of rainfall distributed throughout the year. Brazil's Amazon region and the tropical rainforest of West Africa are examples.

B. SAVANNA: High temperature all during the year with most rainfall in the high sun season. Savanna is sometimes called "tropical wet-and-dry climate." East Africa's lion country and highland Venezuela are examples.

C. DESERT: Desert areas average less than 10 inches of rain a year. The air temperatures are quite high during most of the year. The Sahara and Arabian deserts are examples.

II. MIDDLE LATITUDE CLIMATES (30° to 60°)

A. MEDITERRANEAN: Rainfall occurs during the winter season which is mild. Summers are hot and dry. This climate type is found mainly in lands around the Mediterranean Sea.

B. HUMID SUBTROPICAL: Abundant rainfall during the summer and ample rainfall in the winter. Summers are very warm and temperatures are mild during the rest of the year. Southern Florida and Cuba are examples.

C. MARINE: Often found on the west coasts of continents, this climate
                            has a steady supply of moisture throughout the year.
                            Temperatures are moderate. The Pacific Northwest coast of
                            the United States would be an example.

D. HUMID CONTINENTAL: Found in the Northern Hemisphere, this climate has
                            warm to hot summers and cold winters, with moderate
                            precipitation throughout the year. The state of Iowa and the
                            Ukraine would be examples.

E. DESERT: In the middle latitudes, deserts are quite hot during most of
                            the year. The Sonora Desert of Mexico and Arizona is an example.

III. HIGH LATITUDE CLIMATES (60° to 90°)

A. SUB-ARCTIC: Long cold winters with short but often hot summers.
                            The "taiga" forest belt of the Soviet Union is an example.

B. TUNDRA: Short cool summer, but the land is permanently frozen except
                            for the very top surface for a short time during the year.
                            Northern Siberia is an example.

C. POLAR ICE CAP: Permanent ice forms a polar cap at both the North and
                            South Poles.

IV. HIGH ALTITUDE CLIMATE:

For about every 400 feet in altitude from sea level, the air temperature drops one degree of Fahrenheit. At high altitudes, even on the Equator, polar like conditions exist.

CLOUD

A mass of small water drops or ice crystals, formed by the
condensation of the water vapor in the *atmosphere*.

CIRRUS

35,000'

30,000'

25,000'

ALTOCUMULUS

20,000'

STRATOCUMULUS

15,000'

CUMULUS

10,000'

STRATOS

5,000'

SEA LEVEL

CONFLUENCE

The point at which one *stream* flows into another, or where two
streams converge and unite.

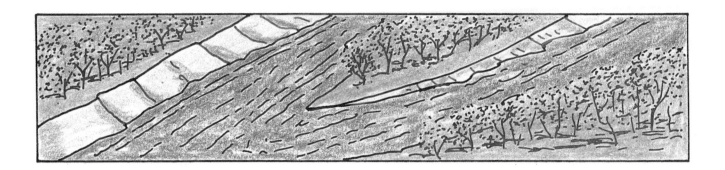

CONTINENT

One of the larger, unbroken masses of land into which the *earth's*
surface is divided: Europe, Asia, Africa, North and South America,
Australia, and Antarctica

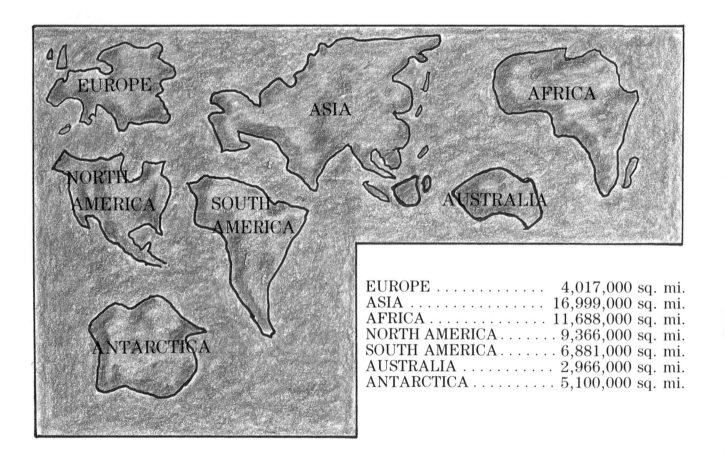

EUROPE	4,017,000 sq. mi.
ASIA	16,999,000 sq. mi.
AFRICA	11,688,000 sq. mi.
NORTH AMERICA	9,366,000 sq. mi.
SOUTH AMERICA	6,881,000 sq. mi.
AUSTRALIA	2,966,000 sq. mi.
ANTARCTICA	5,100,000 sq. mi.

CONTINENTAL DIVIDE

A line which separates the *rivers* flowing towards opposite sides
of a *continent*. In North America the Rocky Mountains cause water
to drain in an easterly or westerly direction. The easterly
flowing waters reach the Atlantic Ocean chiefly through the *Gulf*
of Mexico, and the westerly flowing waters reach the Pacific Ocean
through the Columbia River, or through the Colorado River which
flows into the *Gulf* of California.

CROSS SECTION OF USA

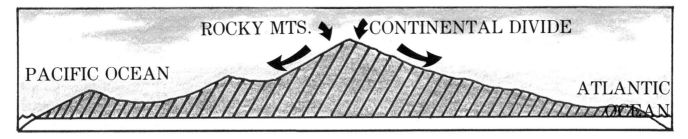

CONTINENTAL SHELF

The *sea* bed, bordering the *continents*, which is covered by shallow water.

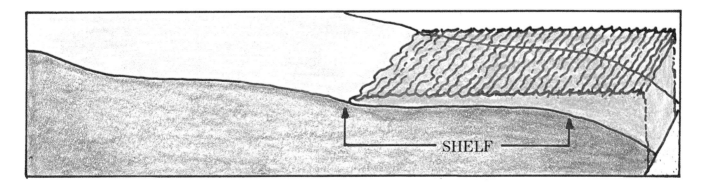

CONTINENTAL SLOPE

The steep slope which descends from the edge of the *continental
shelf* to the deep *ocean* bed.

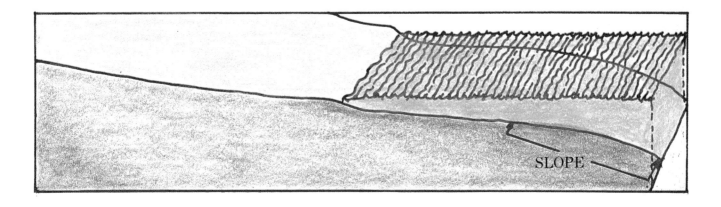

COVE

A small sheltered inlet or *bay*

CONTOUR LINE

A line drawn on a map to join all places at the same height above *sea* level

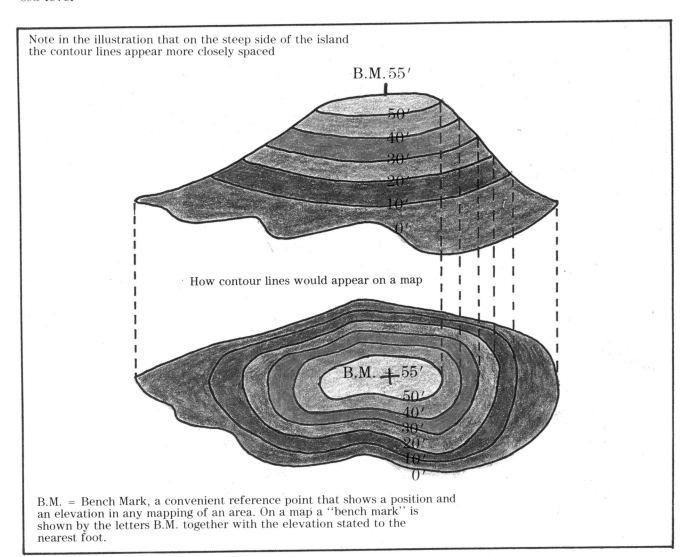

Note in the illustration that on the steep side of the island the contour lines appear more closely spaced

B.M. 55'

50'
40'
30'
20'
10'
0'

How contour lines would appear on a map

B.M. + 55'
50'
40'
30'
20'
10'
0'

B.M. = Bench Mark, a convenient reference point that shows a position and an elevation in any mapping of an area. On a map a "bench mark" is shown by the letters B.M. together with the elevation stated to the nearest foot.

CRATER

The funnel-shaped hollow at the top of the cone of a *volcano*.

CREVASSE

A deep vertical crack in a *glacier*.

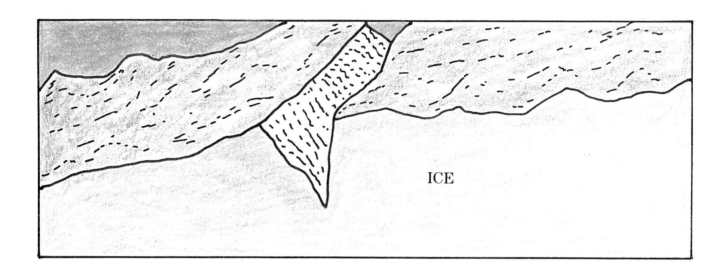

ICE

CRUST (EARTH'S)

The outer part of the *lithosphere*

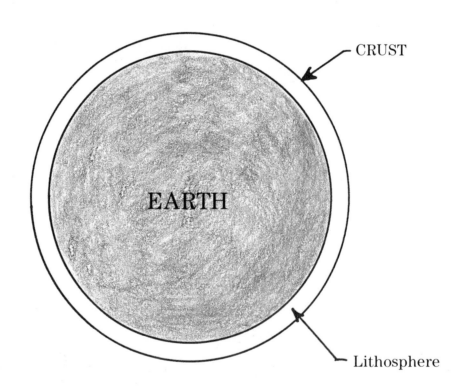

CRUST

EARTH

Lithosphere

CYCLONE

A region of low *atmospheric* pressure. The storm characteristic of a *cyclone* is accompanied by dense black clouds, torrential rain, and often thunder and lightning. Cyclonic winds circulate in a counter clockwise direction in the Northern *Hemisphere* and a clockwise direction in the Southern *Hemisphere*.

DEEP (TRENCH)

One of the deepest parts of the *ocean*, forming a depression in the *sea* floor of limited area and having relatively steep sides.

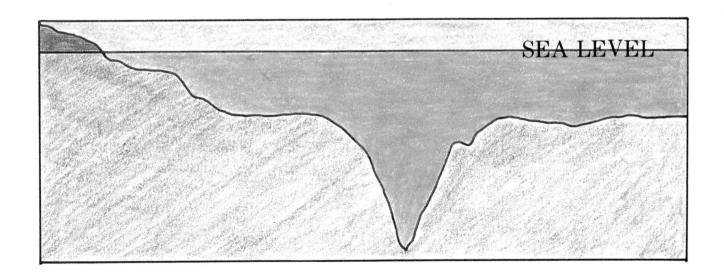

DELL

A small wooded *valley*.

DELTA

The fan-shaped *alluvial* tract formed at the mouth of a *river*.

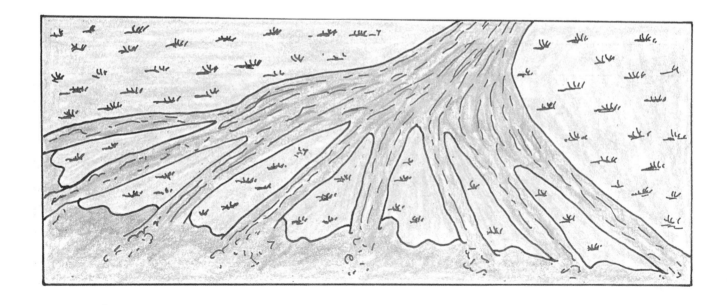

DESERT

An almost barren tract of land in which precipitation is so small
that it will not adequately support vegetation.

SOME OF THE WORLD'S IMPORTANT DESERTS

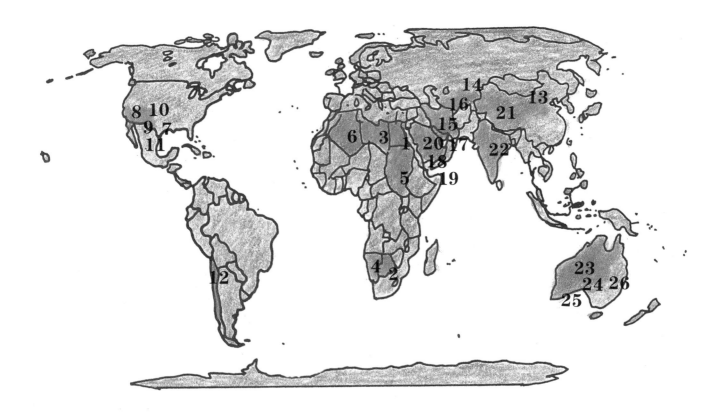

IMPORTANT DESERTS OF THE WORLD

NAME	AREA/EXTENT	LOCATION
AFRICA		
1. ARABIAN	70,000 sq. mi.	Egypt between the Nile River and the Red Sea, extending southward into Sudan
2. KALAHARI	225,000 sq. mi.	Southern Africa
3. LIBYAN	450,000 sq. mi.	Extending from Lybia through southwestern Egypt into Sudan.
4. NAMIB	800 miles in extent	It stretches along the coast of southwest Africa
5. NUBIAN	100,000 sq. mi.	Northeastern Sudan
6. SAHARA	3,500,000 sq. mi.	North Africa, from the Atlantic Coast to the Nile River
NORTH AMERICA		
7. CHIHUAHUAN	140,000 sq. mi.	Texas, New Mexico, Arizona, and Mexico
8. DEATH VALLEY	3,300 sq. mi.	Eastern California and southwestern Nevada
9. MOJAVE	15,000 sq. mi.	Southern California
10. PAINTED DESERT	150 sq. mi.	High *plateau* area in Northern Arizona
11. SONORAN	70,000 sq. mi.	Southwestern Arizona and southeastern California extend into Mexico
SOUTH AMERICA		
12. ATACAMA	600 miles long	Northern Chile
ASIA		
13. GOBI	500,000 sq. mi.	Mongolia and China
14. KARA-KUM	120,000 sq. mi.	Turkmen S.S.R.
15. KAVIR (DASHT-E-KAVIR)	400 miles long	Central Iran
16. KYZYL'KUM	100,000 sq. mi.	Kazakh S.S.R. and Uzbek S.S.R
17. LUT (DASHT-E-LUT)	20,000 sq. mi.	Eastern Iran
18. NAFUD (AN NAFUD)	40,000 sq. mi.	Saudi Arabia
19. RUB AL KHALI	250,000 sq. mi.	South Arabian peninsula
20. SYRIAN	100,000 sq. mi.	Northern Saudi Arabia, eastern Jordan, southern Syria, and western Iraq
21. TAKLIMAKAN	140,000 sq. mi.	Sinkiang Province, China
22. THAR (GREAT INDIAN)	100,000 sq. mi.	India/Pakistan border
AUSTRALIA		
23. GIBSON	120,000 sq. mi.	Western Australia
24. GREAT SANDY	150,000 sq. mi.	Western Australia
25. GREAT VICTORIA	150,000 sq. mi.	Western and southern Australia
26. SIMPSON	40,000 sq. mi.	Central Australia

DISTRIBUTARY

A branch of a *stream* which flows away from the main *channel* without returning to it.

DOLDRUMS

The equatorial belt of low atmospheric pressure where the northeast and southeast *trade winds* converge on and meet each other, producing calms and light surface *winds* and a strong upward movement of air. This region was dreaded by the crews of sailing vessels.

GENERALIZED DIAGRAM OF WIND DIRECTIONS AT THE BOTTOM OF THE ATMOSPHERE

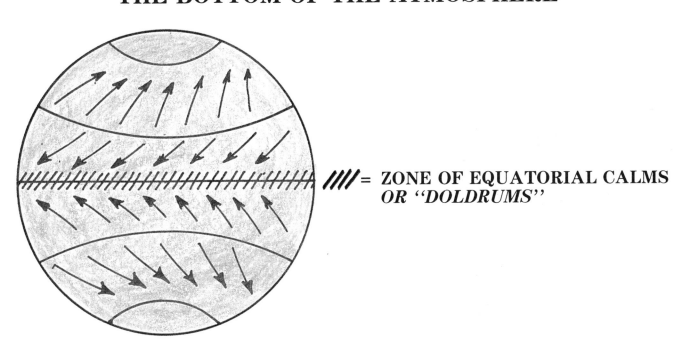

//// = ZONE OF EQUATORIAL CALMS OR "DOLDRUMS"

DUNE

A *hill* of *wind*-blown sand

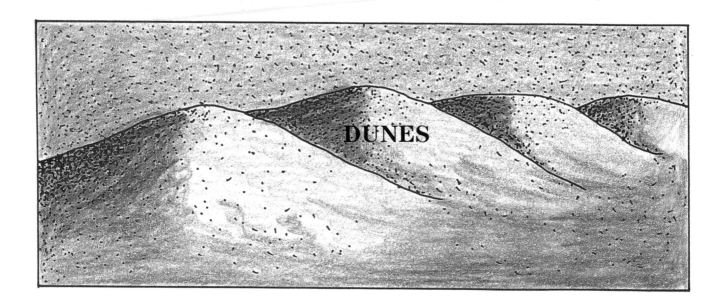

DRUMLIN

A smoothy rounded oval *hill* consisting of *glacial* till*

*till = a mixture of rock fragments ranging in size from clay to boulders and
deposited directly from the ice without water transport

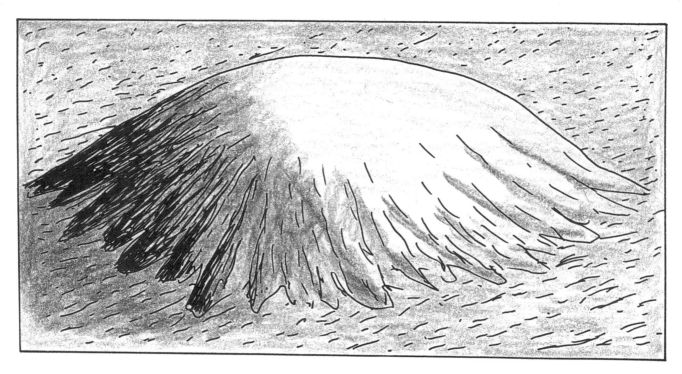

EARTH

The third planet from the sun.

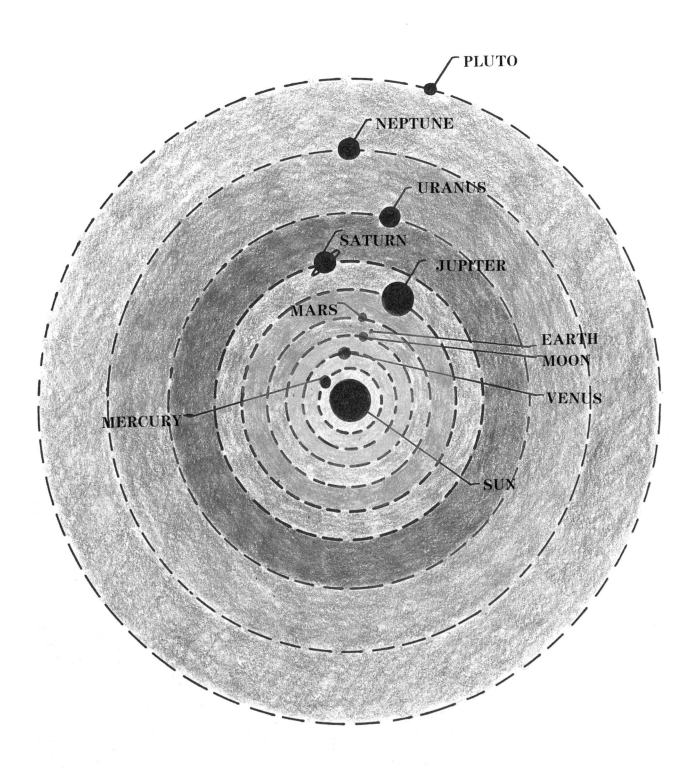

EQUATOR

The imaginary circle, lying between the *poles*, formed at the surface of the *earth* by a plane drawn through the center perpendicular to its *axis*.

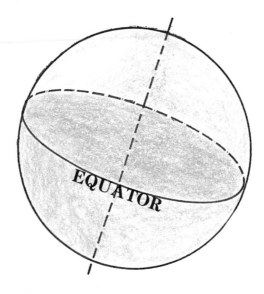

EROSION

The process by which earthy or rock material is removed from any part of the *earth's* surface.

TEARING DOWN LAND FORMS

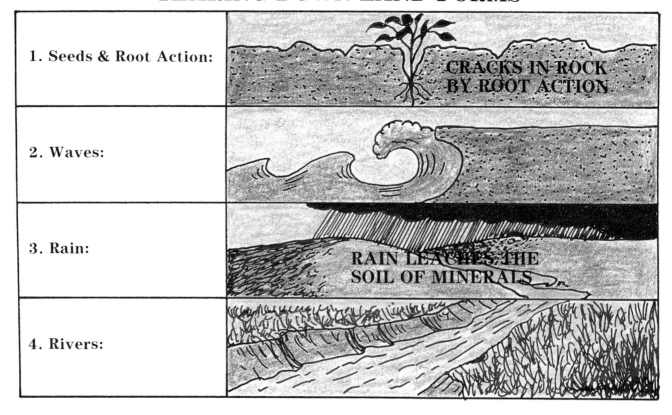

1. Seeds & Root Action:	CRACKS IN ROCK BY ROOT ACTION
2. Waves:	
3. Rain:	RAIN LEACHES THE SOIL OF MINERALS
4. Rivers:	

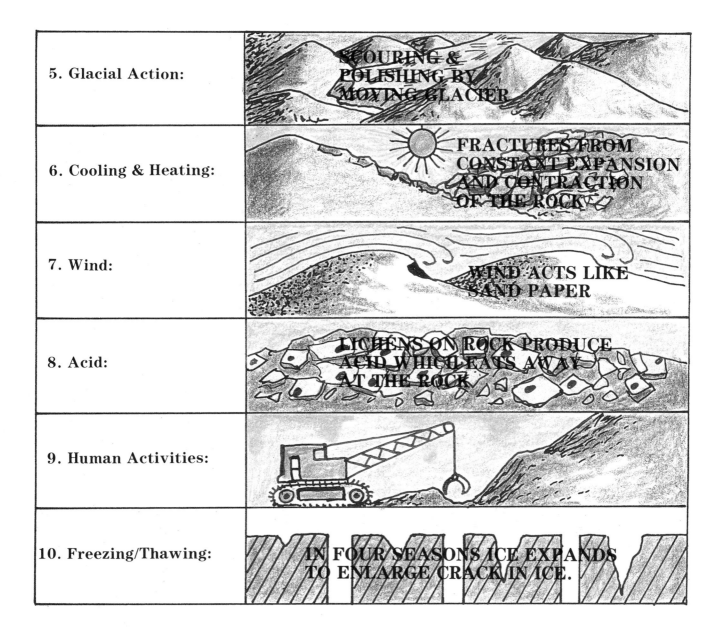

5. Glacial Action:	SCOURING & POLISHING BY MOVING GLACIER
6. Cooling & Heating:	FRACTURES FROM CONSTANT EXPANSION AND CONTRACTION OF THE ROCK
7. Wind:	WIND ACTS LIKE SAND PAPER
8. Acid:	LICHENS ON ROCK PRODUCE ACID WHICH EATS AWAY AT THE ROCK
9. Human Activities:	
10. Freezing/Thawing:	IN FOUR SEASONS ICE EXPANDS TO ENLARGE CRACK IN ICE.

ESCARPMENT

The inland *cliff* or steep slope, formed by the *erosion* of inclined
strata of hard rocks, or as a result of a *fault.*

ESTUARY

The mouth of a *river* where tidal effects are evident, and where
fresh water and *sea* water mix.

FRESH WATER

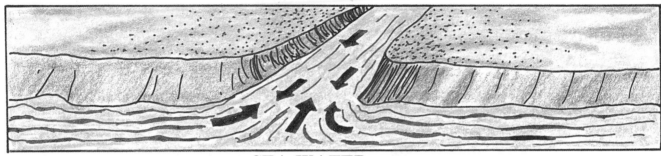

SEA WATER

FAULT

A fracture in the *earth's crust* along which movement has taken place,
and where the rock strata on the two sides do not match.

FIORD (FJORD)

A long narrow inlet into the seacoast, with more or less steep sides.
Examples can be seen in Norway and Alaska.

FLOODPLAIN

The part of any *stream valley* which is inundated during floods

FLOODPLAIN

RIVER

RIVER AT FLOOD STAGE

FRIGID ZONE

The regions within the *Arctic Circle* and the *Antarctic Circle*.

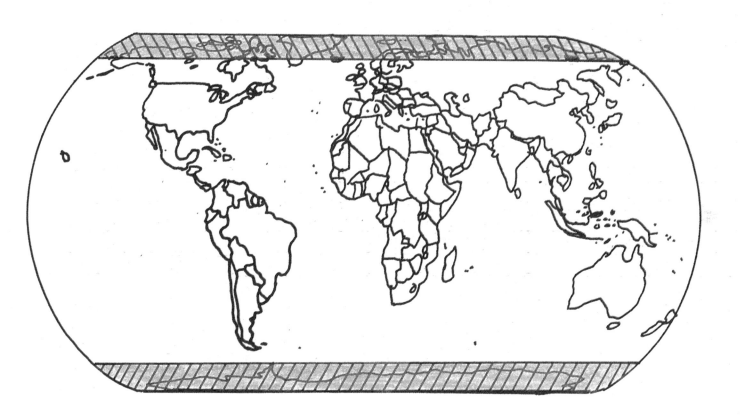

FRONT

The zone where contrasting air masses meet.

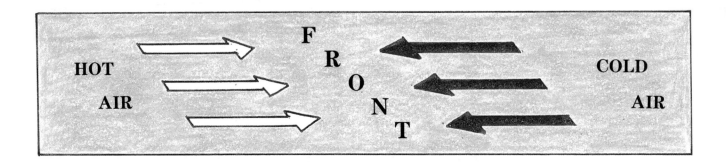

GEYSER

A hot spring which at regular or irregular intervals throws a jet of hot water and steam into the air.

GLACIER

A mass of ice which moves slowly down a *valley* from above the snowline towards the *sea* under the force of gravity.

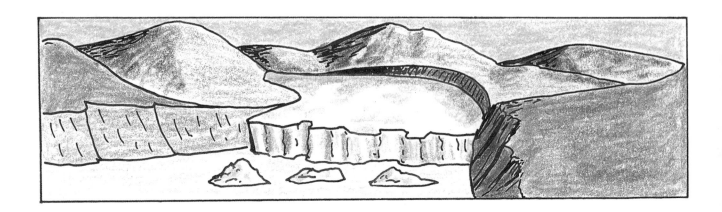

GLEN

A secluded narrow *valley*

GORGE

A synonym for *canyon;* see canyon.

GRASSLANDS

An area of grass or grasslike vegetation. Some common names of grassland areas; Pampas (Argentina), prairie (central North America), llanos (Latin American term for grasslands), steppe (grasslands of the Soviet Union), veld (South African grasslands).

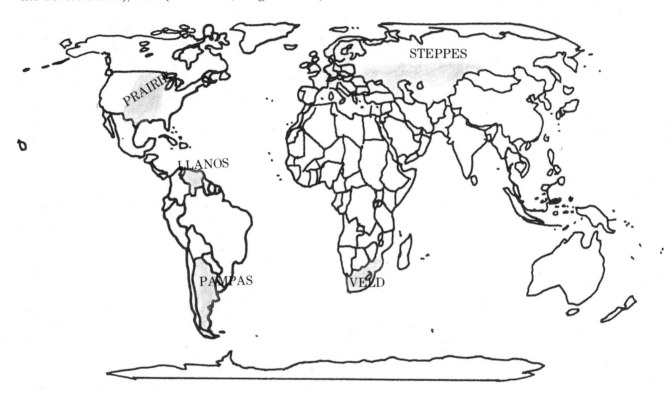

GREAT CIRCLE

A Circle on the *earth's* surface whose plane passes through its center and therefore bisects it into two *hemispheres.*

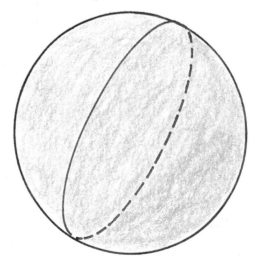

GROIN

A low wall, built on a *beach*, that crosses the shoreline at a right angle.

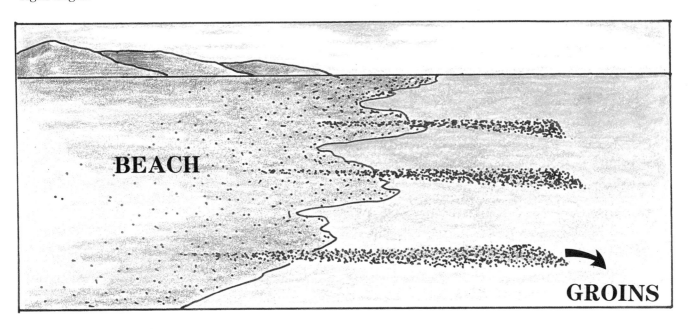

GULF

A large deep *bay*; an extensive inlet penetrating far into the land.

Some Important Gulfs:

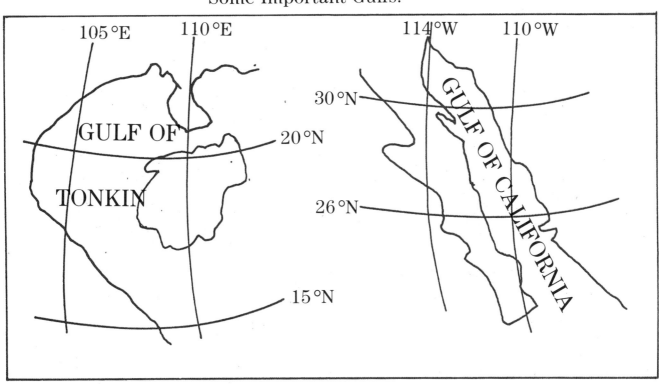

GUYOT

A *seamount* with a conspicuously flat top well below *sea* level

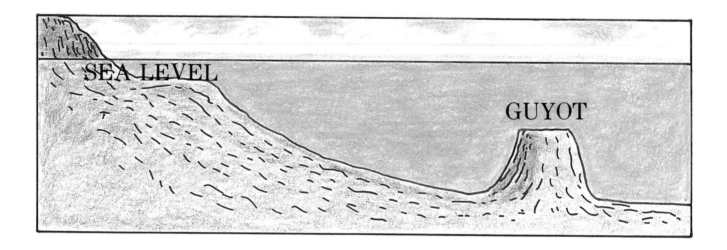

HEMISPHERE

The half of the *earth's* surface, formed when a plane through its center bisects the *earth*.

A vertical cut separating the New World from the Old World creates a Western and an Eastern Hemisphere.

A horizontal cut at the *Equator* creates a Northern Hemisphere and a Southern Hemisphere

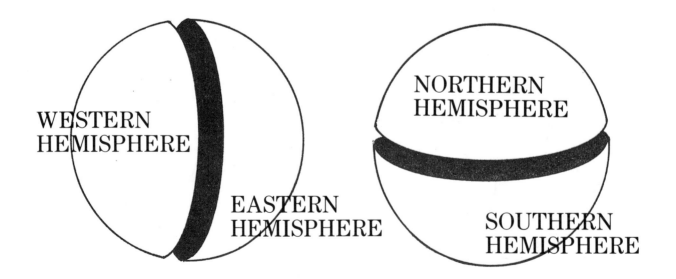

HEADLAND

A point of land, usually
high and with a sheer drop
extending out into a body of
water.

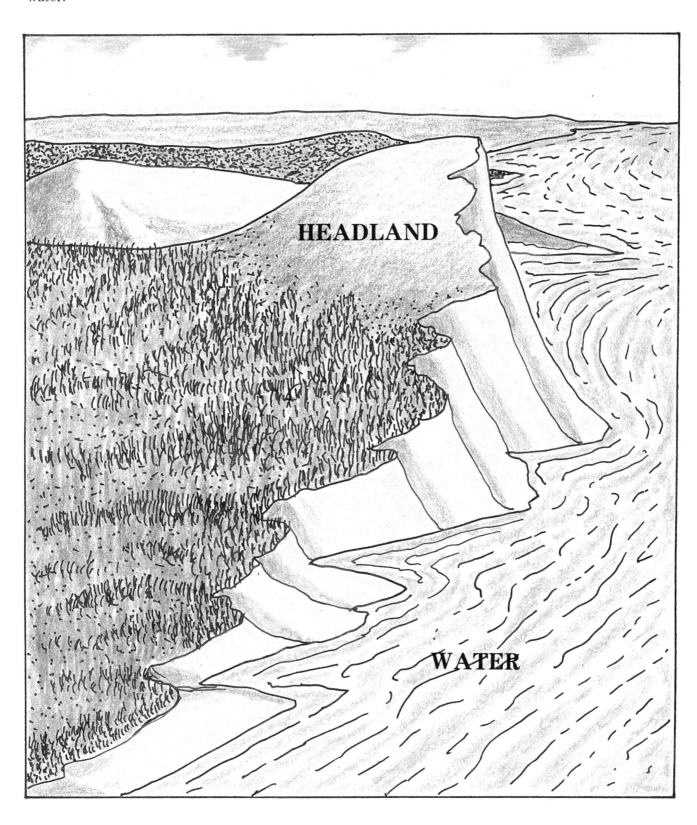

ICEBERG

A mass of land ice which has been broken off from the end of a *glacier* or from an ice barrier, and is afloat in the *sea*.

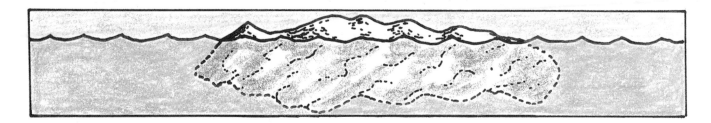

ICE FLOE

A large, flat mass of floating *sea* ice.

INTERNATIONAL DATELINE

The line approximating the *meridian* 180° where the date changes by exactly one day as it is crossed.

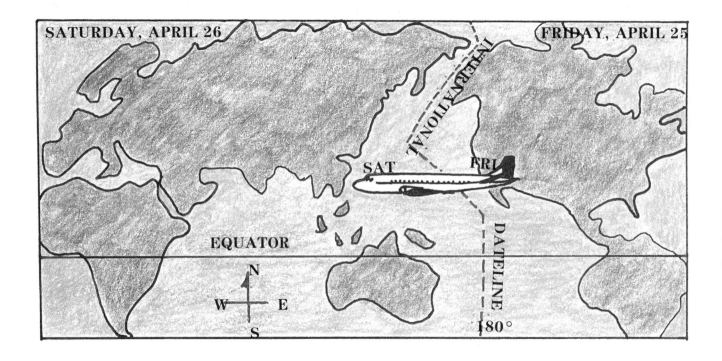

HILL

A well-defined naturally elevated area of land smaller than a
mountain but larger than a hillock.

HILLOCK HILL MOUNTAIN

HURRICANE

A *cyclone* in the West Indies with *wind* speeds of more than 75
miles per hour.

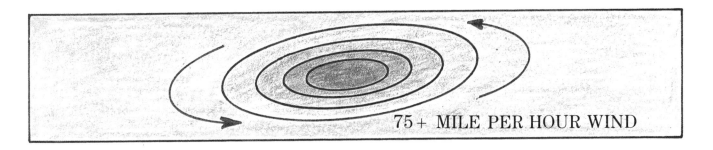

75+ MILE PER HOUR WIND

HYDROSPHERE

The water areas of the *earth* including the *oceans, lakes,
streams,* ground water, snow and ice.

"most of the earth's hydrosphere is in the southern hemisphere"

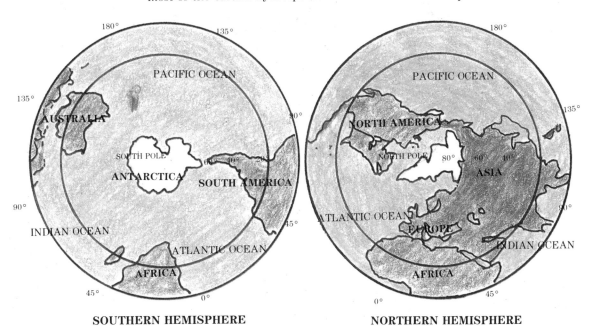

SOUTHERN HEMISPHERE   **NORTHERN HEMISPHERE**

ISLAND

A land mass, especially one smaller than a *continent*, entirely surrounded by water.

THE TEN LARGEST ISLANDS IN THE WORLD

1. Greenland . . . . 840,000 sq. mi.
   (Denmark)
2. New Guinea . . . . 306,000 sq. mi.
   (Indo./Papua, New Guinea)
3. Borneo . . . . 280,000 sq. mi.
   (Indo./Malaysia)
4. Madagascar . . . . 226,658 sq. mi.
5. Baffin . . . . 195,928 sq. mi.
   (Canada)
6. Sumatra . . . . 165,000 sq. mi.
   (Indo.)
7. Honshu . . . . 87,805 sq. mi.
   (Japan)
8. Great Britain . . . . 84,200 sq. mi.
9. Victoria . . . . 83,896 sq. mi.
   (Canada)
10. Ellesmere . . . . 75,767 sq. mi.
    (Canada)

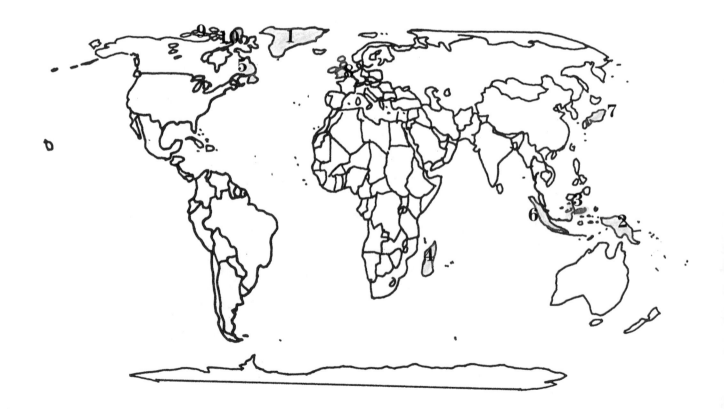

ISTHMUS

A narrow strip of land joining two large land areas.

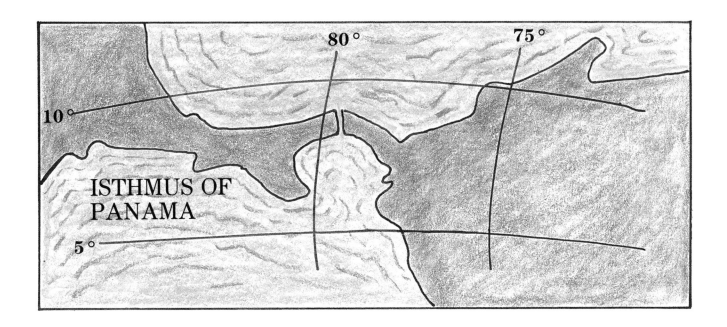

IMPORTANT ISTHMUSES IN THE WORLD

1. Isthmus of Chinecto . . . . Connects Nova Scotia and New Brunswick, Canada
2. Rae Isthmus . . . . Connects Melville Peninsula with the main territory of the District of Keewatin, Northern Territories, Canada
3. Isthmus of Tehuantepec . . . . Connects Central America and the Yucatan Peninsula with the main area of Mexico
4. Isthmus of Panama . . . . Connects North and South America
5. Isthmus of Kra . . . . Connects the Malay Peninsula with the Indochina Peninsula

JET STREAM

A high speed *wind* near the *troposphere* (see *atmosphere)*,
generally moving from a westerly direction at speeds often
exceeding 20 miles an hour.

KNOLL

A small, rounded *hill* or mound

LAGOON

A shallow stretch of water which is partly or completely
separated from the *sea* by a narrow strip of land

LAKE

A large inland body of fresh or salt water

THE WORLD'S TOP TEN LAKES IN AREA

NAME	LOCATION	AREA
1. Caspian Sea	Asia-Europe	143,244 sq. mi.
2. Superior	North America	31,700 sq. mi.
3. Victoria	Africa	26,828 sq. mi.
4. Aral Sea	Asia	24,904 sq. mi.
5. Huron	North America	23,000 sq. mi.
6. Michigan	North America	22,300 sq. mi.
7. Tanganyka	Africa	12,700 sq. mi.
8. Baykal	Asia	12,162 sq. mi.
9. Great Bear	North America	12,096 sq. mi.
10. Malawi	Africa	11,150 sq. mi.

THE WORLD'S TOP TEN LAKES IN AREA

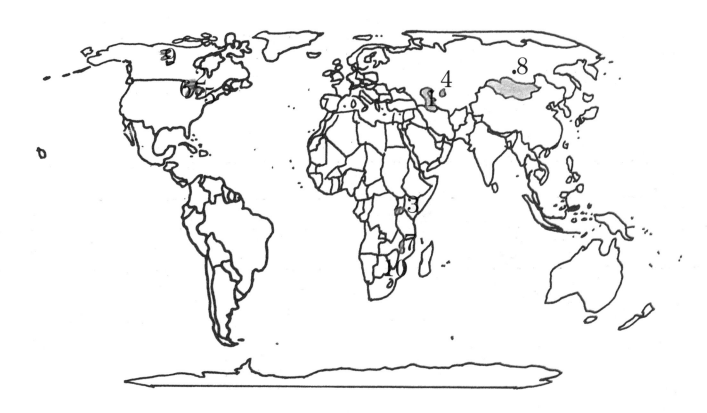

LATITUDE

The angular distance of a point on the *earth's* surface north or south of the *equator,* as measured from the center of the *earth*.

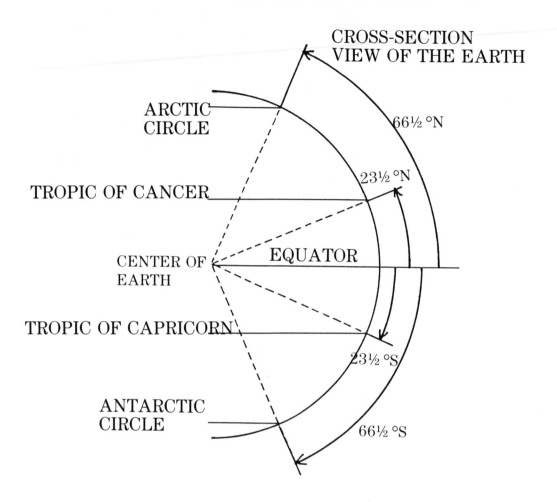

CROSS-SECTION
VIEW OF THE EARTH

ARCTIC
CIRCLE

66½ °N

TROPIC OF CANCER

23½ °N

CENTER OF
EARTH

EQUATOR

TROPIC OF CAPRICORN

23½ °S

ANTARCTIC
CIRCLE

66½ °S

LEEWARD

The side away from the *wind*

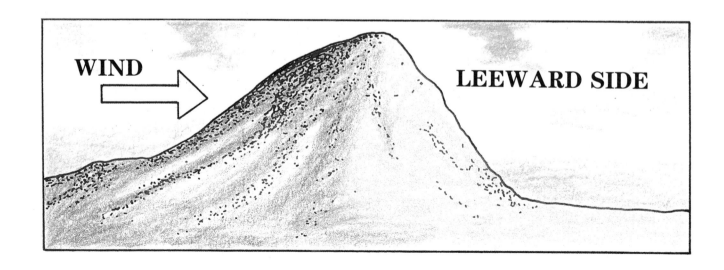

WIND

LEEWARD SIDE

LEVEE

The natural bank of a *river* formed during flooding by the
deposition of sediment

LITHOSPHERE

The outer zone of the solid *earth*

LONGITUDE

The angular distance, measured along the *equator*, between the
meridian through a given point and a standard or *prime meridian*

**EXAMPLE
OF
LONGITUDE**

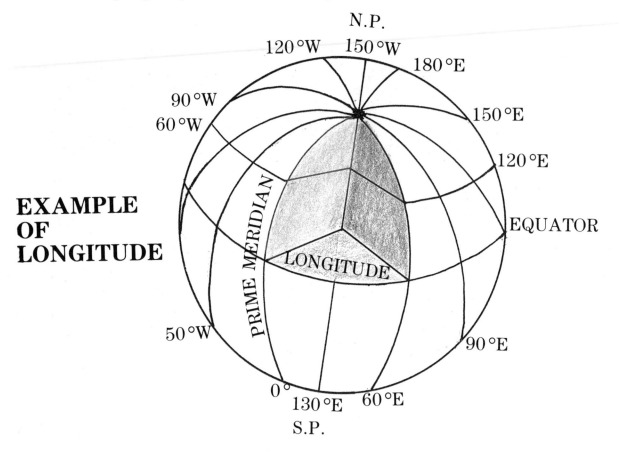

MASSIF

A large *mountain* mass or compact group of connected *mountains*
forming an independent portion of a *range*

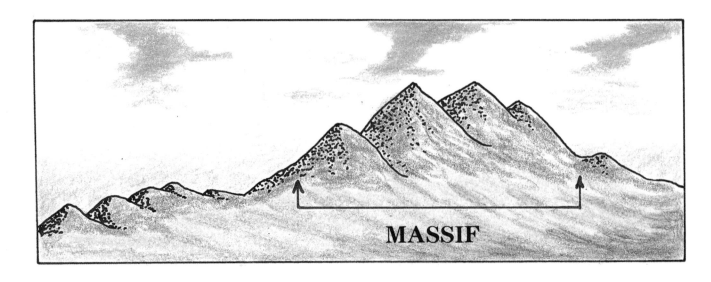

MEANDER

A winding course of a *river*

MERIDIAN

A line of *longitude*

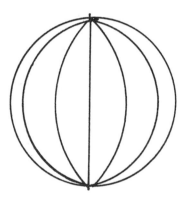

MESA

A flat, table-like mass, which falls away steeply on all sides

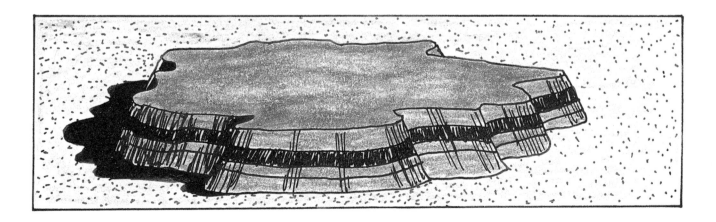

MORAINE

An accumulation of boulders, stones, or other debris carried and deposited by a *glacier*

MONSOON

The type of *wind* system in which there is a complete or almost complete reversal of prevailing direction from *season* to *season*.

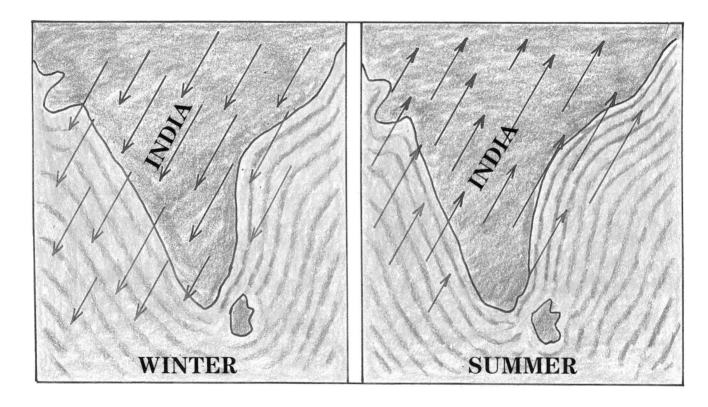

MOUNTAIN

A mass of land considerably higher than its surroundings

THE HIGHEST MOUNTAINS IN THE WORLD'S SEVEN CONTINENTS
(1) ASIA - Mt. Everest (29,028′)   (2) SOUTH AMERICA - Mt. Aconcagua (22,834′)

(3) NORTH AMERICA - Mt. McKinley (20,320′)   (4) AFRICA - Mt. Kilimanjaro (19,340′)

(5) EUROPE - Mt. El'brus (18,510′)   (6) ANTARCTICA - Vinson Massif (16,864′)

(7) AUSTRALIA - Mt. Kosciusko (7,310′)

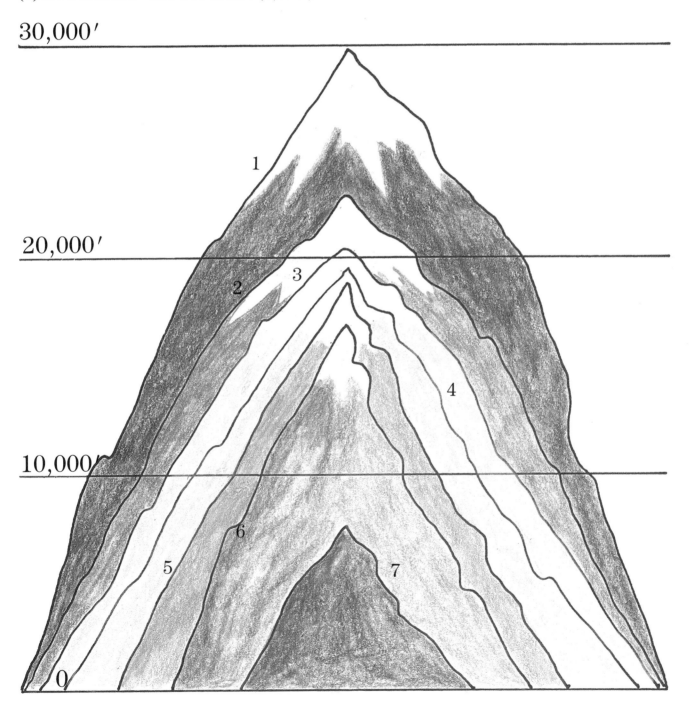

30,000′

20,000′

10,000′

MOUNTAIN RANGE

A chain of *mountains*

NORTH POLE

The northern end of the *earth's axis* of rotation

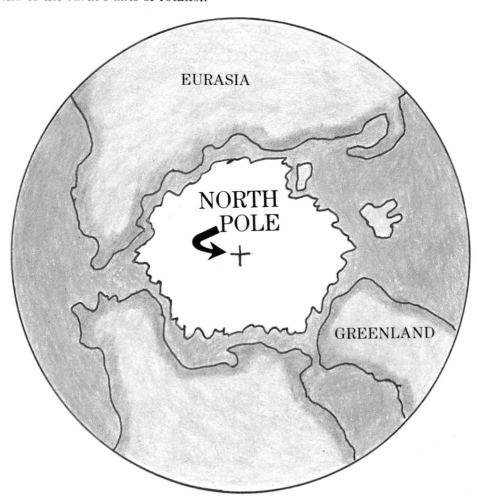

OASIS

An area in the midst of a *desert,* which is made fertile by
the presence of water

OCEAN

The sheet of salt water surrounding the *continents* and divided
by them into several extensive portions each known as an ocean.

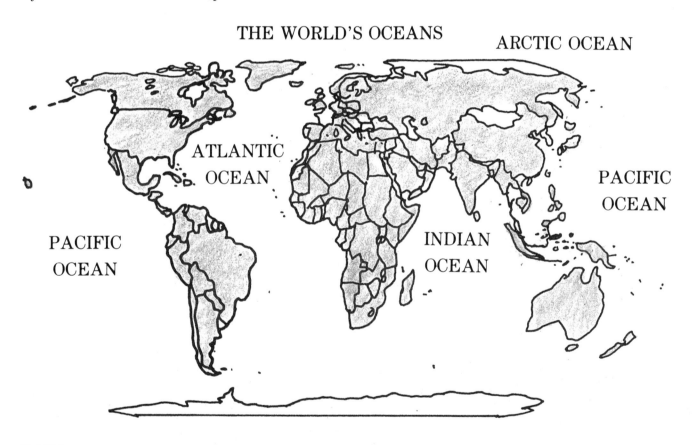

THE WORLD'S OCEANS

DATA:

	AREA (SQ.MI.)	AVERAGE DEPTH IN FEET
PACIFIC	64,186,300	12,925
ATLANTIC	33,420,000	11,730
INDIAN	28,350,500	12,598
ARCTIC	5,105,700	3,407

OCEAN CURRENT

The vertical or horizontal movement of the water of the *ocean*.

SOME MAJOR SURFACE CURRENTS OF THE OCEAN

NAME OF CURRENT	CHARACTERISTICS
1. AGULHAS	WARM
2. ANTILLES	WARM
3. ALASKA	WARM
4. BENGUELA	COLD
5. BRAZIL	WARM
6. CANARIES	WARM
7. CALIFORNIA	COLD
8. CAPE HORN	COLD
9. EAST AUSTRALIA	WARM
10. EAST GREENLAND	COLD
11. EQUATORIAL	WARM
12. FALKLAND	COLD
13. FLORIDA	WARM
14. GUINEA	COLD
15. GULF	WARM
16. HUMBOLDT	COLD
17. KUROSHIO	WARM
18. LABRADOR	COLD
19. NORTH EQUATORIAL	WARM
20. NORWEGIAN	WARM
21. NORTHEAST MONSOON	WARM
22. NORTH ATLANTIC	WARM
23. NORTH PACIFIC	WARM
24. OYASHIO	COLD
25. POLAR	COLD
26. PORTUGAL	WARM
27. SOUTH EQUATORIAL	WARM
28. WEDDELL	COLD
29. WESTWIND DRIFT	COLD

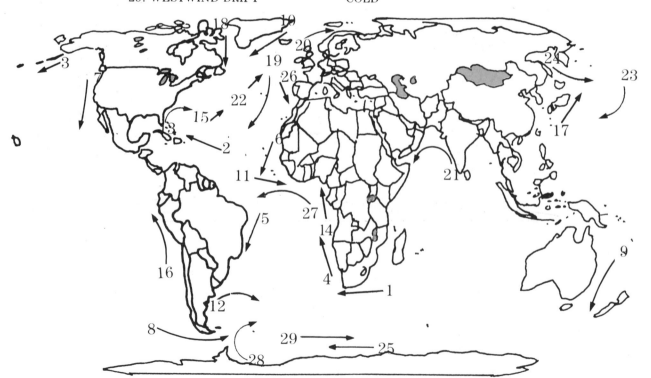

OX-BOW LAKE

A *lake* formed when a *meandering river,* having bent in almost a complete circle, cuts across the narrow neck of land between the two stretches and leaves a back-water, silt is gradually deposited by the *river* at the entrance of this backwater until the latter is finally separated from the *river* and becomes a *lake*

PARALLEL

An east-west line on a globe or map used in measuring *latitude*

IMPORTANT PARALLELS:

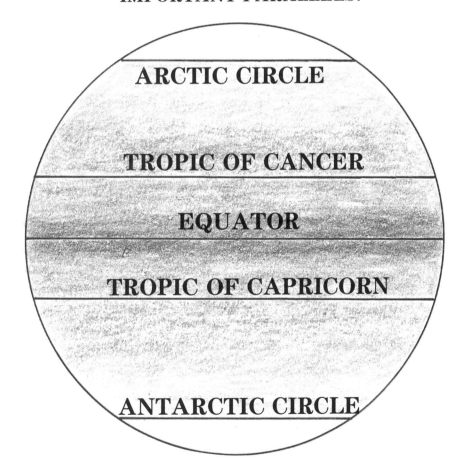

ARCTIC CIRCLE

TROPIC OF CANCER

EQUATOR

TROPIC OF CAPRICORN

ANTARCTIC CIRCLE

PASS

A low and passable gap through a *mountain* barrier

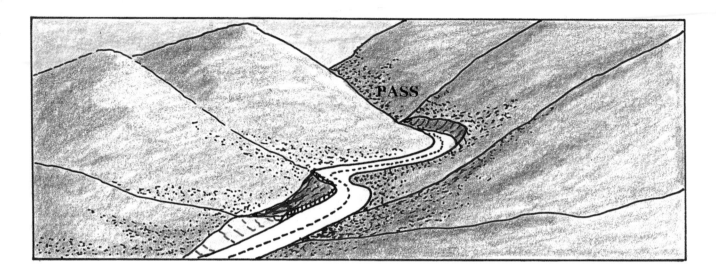

PEDIMENT

A sloping surface, cut across bedrock, adjacent to the base of
a highland in an arid *climate*

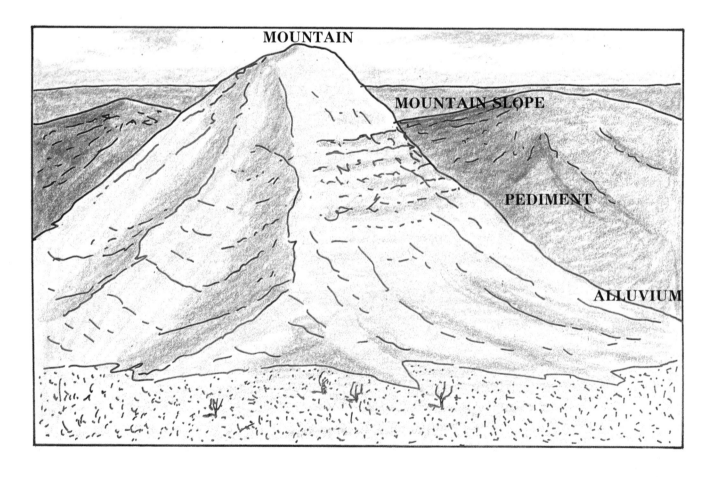

PENEPLAIN

A nearly flat land surface representing an advanced stage
of *erosion*

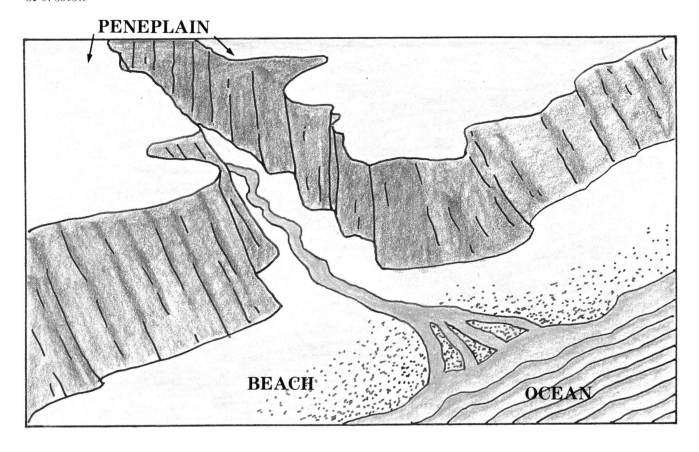

PENINSULA

A stretch of land almost surrounded by water

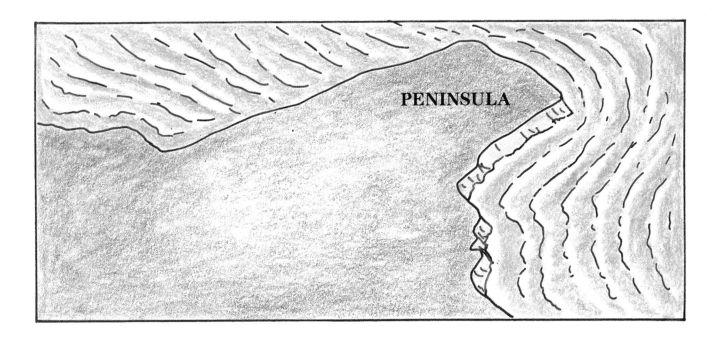

PLAIN

An extensive treeless level land region

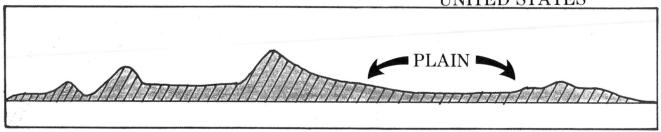

PLAIN

PLATEAU

An extensive, level or mainly level area of elevated land

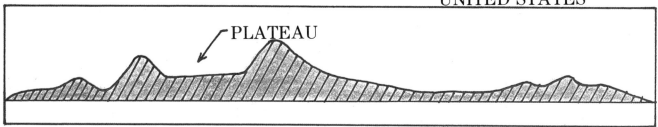

PLATEAU

PLUME

A column of water that rises like chimney smoke from vents in the sea floor

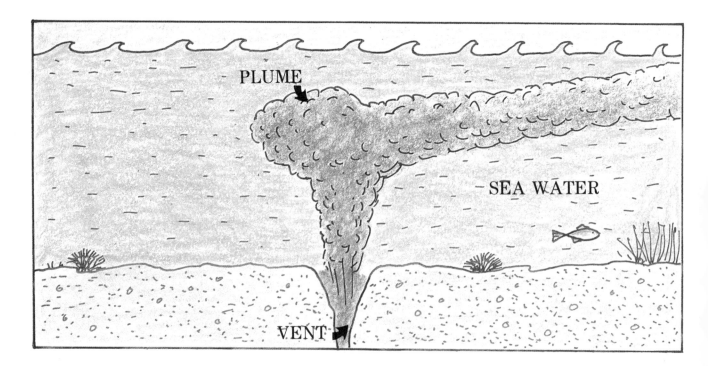

PLUME

SEA WATER

VENT

POINT

A tapering extension of land projecting into the water

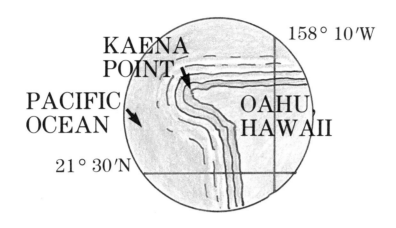

PRIME MERIDIAN

The zero *meridian* from which *longitude* east and west is measured
and which passes through Greenwich, England

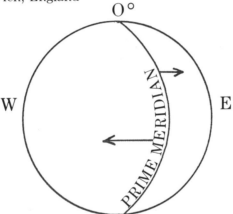

RAPIDS

An extremely fast-moving part of a river, caused by a steep descent in the riverbed.

REEF

A ridge of rocks, lying near the surface of the *sea*, which may be
visible at low *tide*, but is usually covered by water

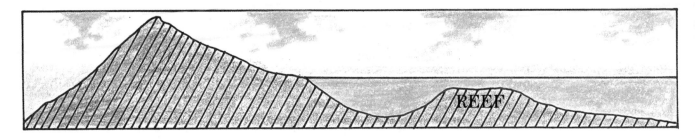

RIFT VALLEY

A *valley* which has been formed by the sinking of land between two
roughly parallel *faults*

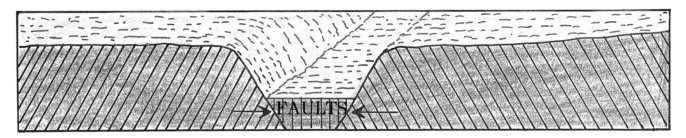

RIVER

A large natural stream of water emptying into an *ocean, lake,*
or other body of water, and usually fed along its course by
converging *tributaries*
The source of a river is where it begins

The mouth of a river
is where it flows into a
larger body of water

THE WORLD'S TEN LONGEST RIVERS

1. Nile . . . . 4,160 miles	6. Congo . . . . 2,900 miles
2. Amazon . . . . 4,000 miles	7. Amur . . . . 2,744 miles
3. Chang Jiang. . . . . 3,964 miles	8. Lena . . . . 2,734 miles
4. Ob-Irtysh . . . . 3,362 miles	9. Mackenzie . . . . 2,635 miles
5. Huang . . . . 2,903 miles	10. Mekong. . . . . 2,600 miles

SEA

One of the smaller divisions of the *oceans;* a large expanse of inland salt water

Some Seas Commonly Found in Atlases:

Name of Sea	Location
1. Adriatic	between Italy and Yugoslavia
2. Aegean	between Turkey and Greece
3. Amundsen	Antarctica
4. Andaman	by Burma and Thailand
5. Arabian	between Arabia and India
6. Arafura	between New Guinea and Australia
7. Aral	south of the Urals in the Soviet Union
8. Balearic	between Spain and the Balearic Islands
9. Baltic	between Sweden and the coasts of Poland and the Soviet Union
10. Banda	north of Timor, Indonesia
11. Barents	off the north coast of Norway and the Soviet Union
12. Beaufort	off the north coast of Alaska
13. Bellingshausen	Antarctica
14. Bering	between Alaska and the Soviet Union
15. Bismarck	off the northeast coast of New Guinea
16. Black	between Turkey and the Soviet Union
17. Caribbean	between the east coast of Central America and the northeast coast of South America
18. Caspian	between Iran and the Soviet Union
19. Celebes	between the Celebes and the Philippines
20. Ceram	north of the island of Ceram, Indonesia
21. Chukchi	between the Soviet Union and Alaska
22. Coral	off the northeast coast of Australia
23. Dead	between Israel and Jordan
24. East China	between Japan and China
25. East Siberian	off the north coast of the Soviet Union
26. Hudson Bay	Canada
27. Inland	between the islands of Shikoku and Honshu Japan
28. Ionian	between Italy and Greece
29. Irish	between Ireland and Great Britain
30. Java	north of the island of Java, Indonesia
31. Kara	off the north coast of the Soviet Union
32. Labrador	between Greenland and Newfoundland
33. Laccadive	off India's southwest coast
34. Laptiev	off the north coast of the Soviet Union

35. Ligurian . . . . off the coast of Genoa, Italy
36. Mindanao . . . . north of the island of Mindanao, the Philippines
37. Molucca . . . . between the Celebes and Moluccas, Indonesia
38. Mediterranean . . . . between Europe and North Africa
39. North . . . . between Great Britain and Denmark
40. Norwegian . . . . between Norway and Iceland
41. Philippine . . . . between Japan and the Philippines
42. Red . . . . between Arabia and Africa
43. Ross . . . . Antarctica
44. Sargasso . . . . between the West Indies and the Azores
45. Sea of Azov . . . . north of the Black Sea
46. Sea of Crete . . . . north of the island of Crete, Greece
47. Sea of Galilee . . . . Israel
48. Sea of Japan . . . . between Japan and Korea
49. Sea of Mamara . . . . between European Turkey and Asiatic Turkey
50. Sea of Okhotsk . . . . between Siberia and Japan
51. Sibuyan . . . . surrounds the island of Sibuyan, the Philippines
52. Solomon . . . . between New Britain and New Guinea
53. South China . . . . by the Philippines, Indonesia, Vietnam and China
54. Sulu . . . . between Borneo and the Philippines
55. Tasman . . . . between New Zealand and Antarctica
56. Timor . . . . south of the island of Timor, Indonesia
57. Tyrrhenian . . . . between Sardinia and the mainland of Italy
58. Visayan . . . . northeast of Panay, the Philippines
59. White . . . . by the Kola Peninsula of the Soviet Union
60. Weddell . . . . Antarctica
61. Yellow . . . . between Korea and China

SOME SEAS COMMONLY FOUND IN ATLASES

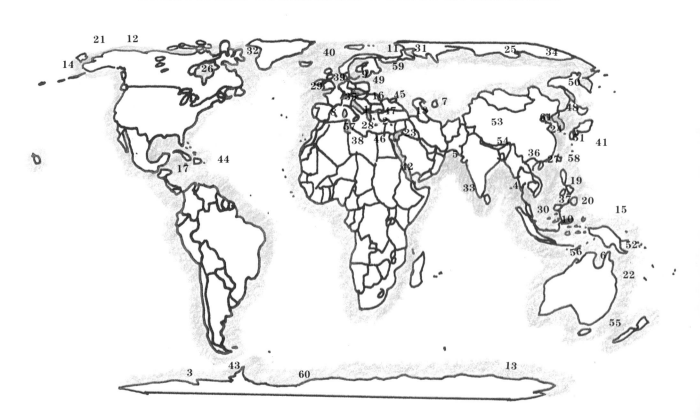

SEA ARCHES

Wave action washes away weaker rock areas producing arches
connecting more solid rock areas to the mainland

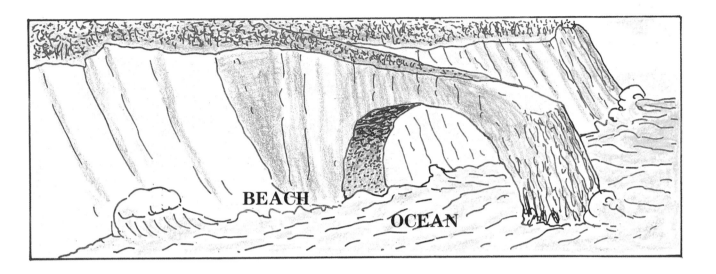

SEA CAVE

A cave found in a coastal area formed by the *erosive* action
of the *sea*

SEAMOUNTS

Isolated submarine *mountains*

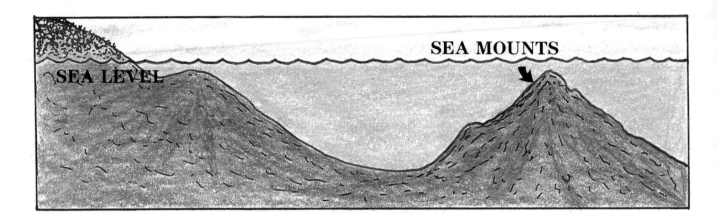

SEASONS

Four equal natural divisions of the year; spring, summer, autumn, and winter, indicated by the passage of the sun through an equinox or solstice and derived from the apparent north-south movement of the sun caused by the fixed direction of the *earth*'s axis in solar orbit

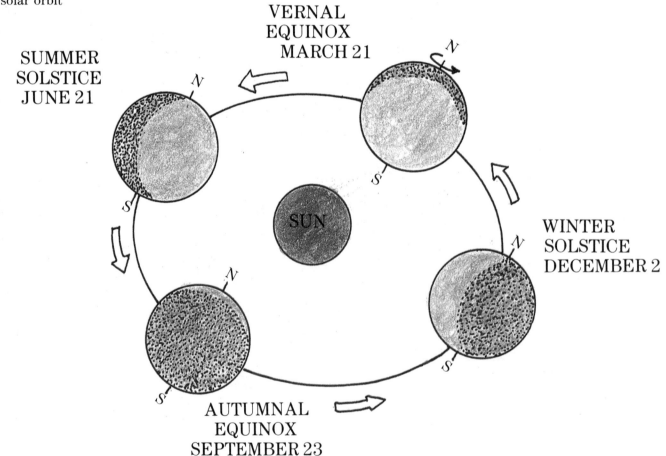

SINK

A large cavity open to the sky generally created by collapse
of a *cavern* roof

SMALL CIRCLE

Any circle on the surface of a sphere or globe which is less than
a *great circle*. All parallels except the *equator* are small circles

SMALL
CIRCLE

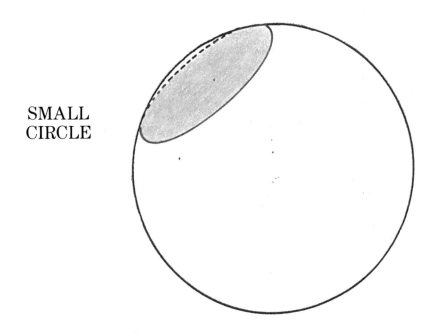

SOUND

A long relatively wide body of water larger than a *strait* or a *channel* connecting larger bodies of water

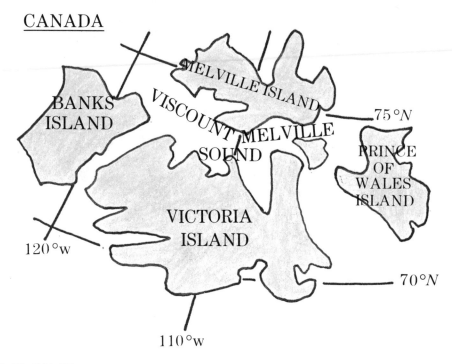

SOUTH POLE

The southern end of the *earth*'s *axis* of rotation

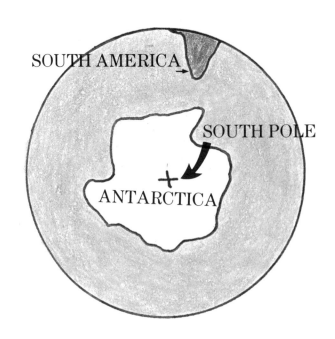

SPIT

A narrow low-lying tongue of sand or gravel projecting into the *sea*

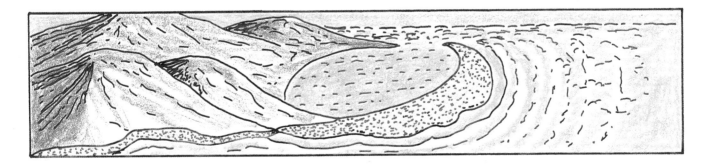

STACK

A rocky islet or pillar, near to a coastline, which has been
isolated by the *erosive* action of the waves

STALACTITE

A column of mineral matter hanging from an elevated point. . . .
often found in limestone caves

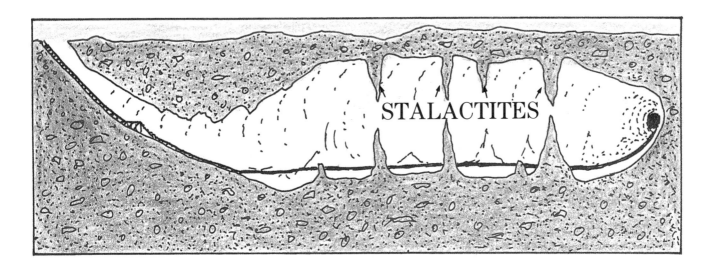

STALAGMITE

A column of calcium carbonate formed on the floor of a cave by drip

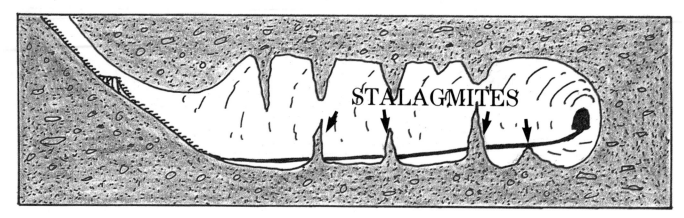

STALAGMITES

STEPPES

See *GRASSLANDS*

STORM

An *atmospheric* disturbance manifested in strong *winds* accompanied by rain, snow, or other precipitation and often by thunder and lightning

Meteorological definitions of some common storms:
Gale: **a wind from 32 to 63 miles per hour**
Storm: **a wind from 64 to 72 miles per hour**
Hurricane (Typhoon): **a wind from 75 to 125+ miles per hour**
Tornado: **wind speeds to 300 miles per hour**

WIND SPEED STORM GRAPH

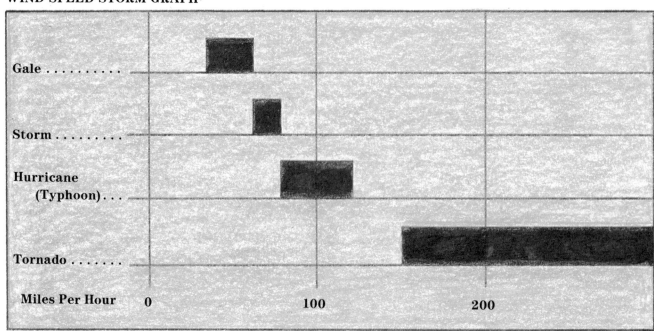

STRAIT

A narrow stretch of *sea* connecting two extensive areas of *sea*

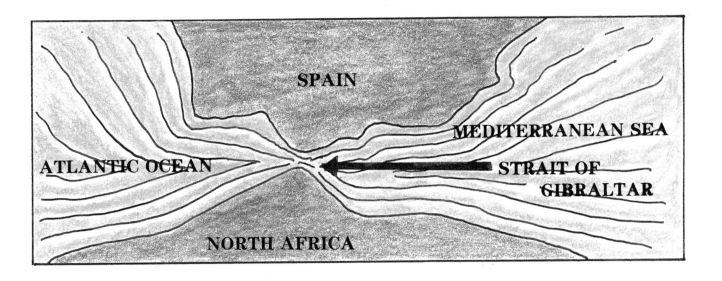

STREAM

A body of running water; especially, such a body moving over the *earth*'s surface in a *channel* or bed, as a brook, rivulet, or *river*

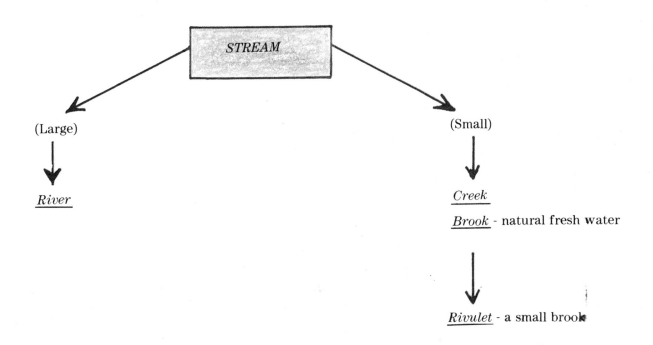

SUMMIT

The highest point on a *mountain*. . . . if the summit is tapered it
is often called a "peak"

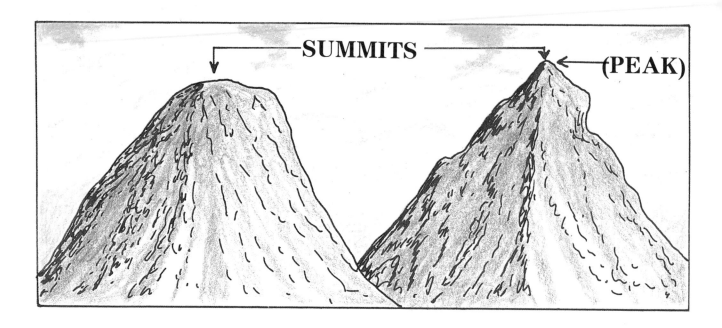

SWAMP

A tract of low-lying land which is saturated with moisture and
usually overgrown with vegetation

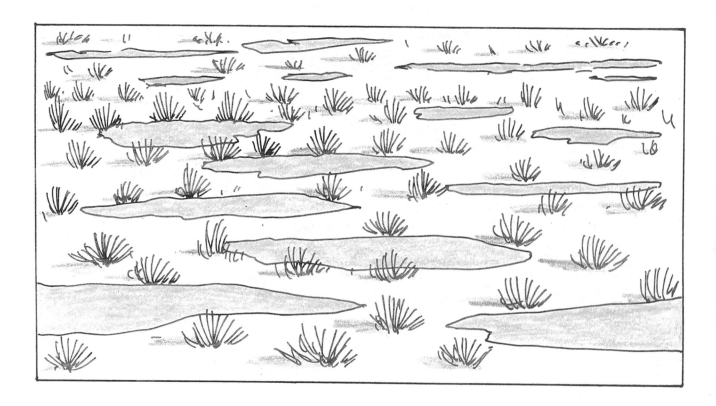

TAIGA

The coniferous forest land of Siberia, bordered on the north by
the treeless, inhospitable *tundra* and on the south by the *steppes*

TAIGA ZONE

TEMPERATE ZONE

The middle *latitudes*, the zone between the *torrid zone* and the
frigid zone; in the northern *hemisphere* between the *Tropic of
Cancer* and the *Arctic Circle*; in the southern *hemisphere* between
the *Tropic of Capricorn* and the *Antarctic Circle*

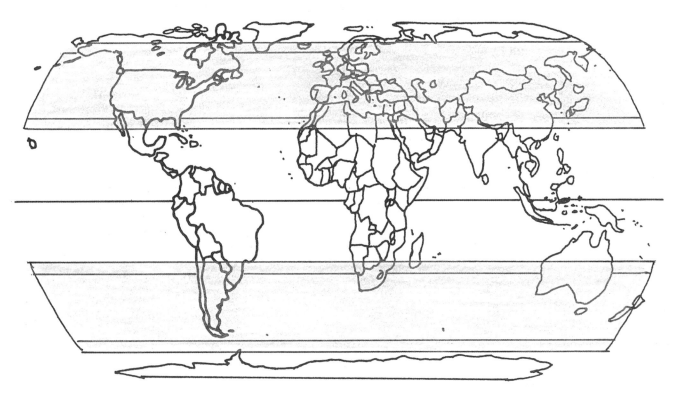

TIDE

The periodic variation in the surface level of the *oceans* and of *bays, gulfs,* inlets and tidal regions of *rivers,* caused by the gravitational attraction of the sun and the moon, the lunar effect being the more powerful.

TIMBERLINE

The upper limit of tree growth in *mountains*

TOMBOLO

A *bar* which joins an *island* to the mainland or joins two *islands*

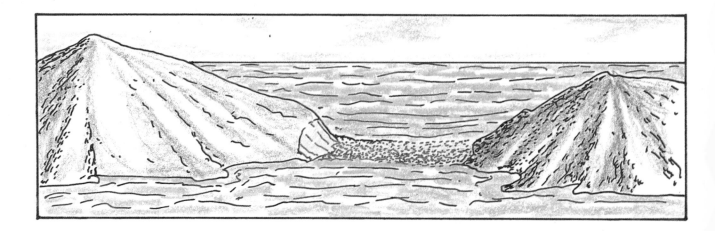

TORNADO

An extremely violent whirlwind covering a relatively small area;
its diameter being usually about one-quarter of a mile; *wind* speeds
can reach 500 miles per hour

TORRID ZONE

The region of the earth's surface between the *Tropic of Cancer* and
the *Tropic of Capricorn*

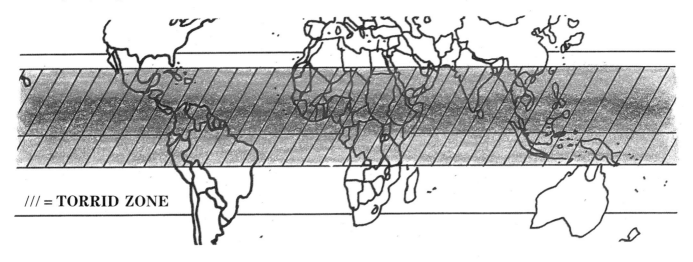

/// = **TORRID ZONE**

TRADE WINDS

The *winds* which blow from the sub-tropical belts of high pressure
towards the *equatorial* region of low pressure; from the northeast
in the Northern *Hemisphere* and from the southeast in the Southern
Hemisphere

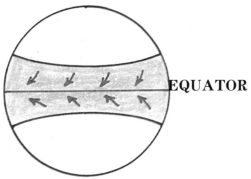

EQUATOR

TRIBUTARY

A *stream* which flows into a larger *stream*

TROPIC OF CANCER

The *parallel* of *latitude* 23½° north of the *equator*

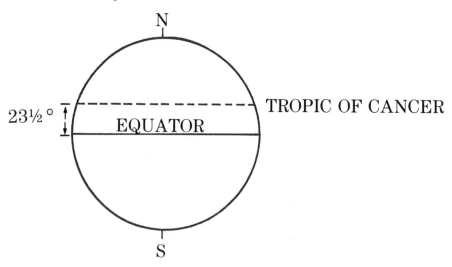

TROPIC OF CAPRICORN

The *parallel* of *latitude* 23½° south of the *equator*

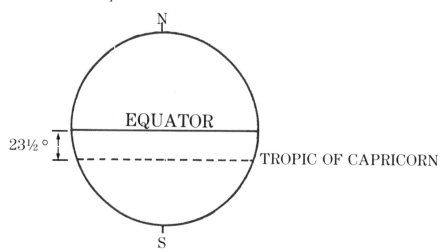

TSUNAMI

A large *sea* wave occasionally experienced along the coasts of
Japan and in other regions, especially in the Pacific Ocean,
caused by an earthquake taking place on the *ocean* bed . . . it
rises to considerable heights as it approaches the coastline

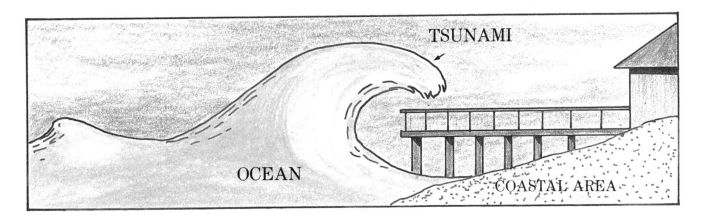

TUNDRA

The treeless *plains* of northern North America and northern
Eurasia lying principally along the *Arctic Circle,* and on
the northern side of the coniferous forests

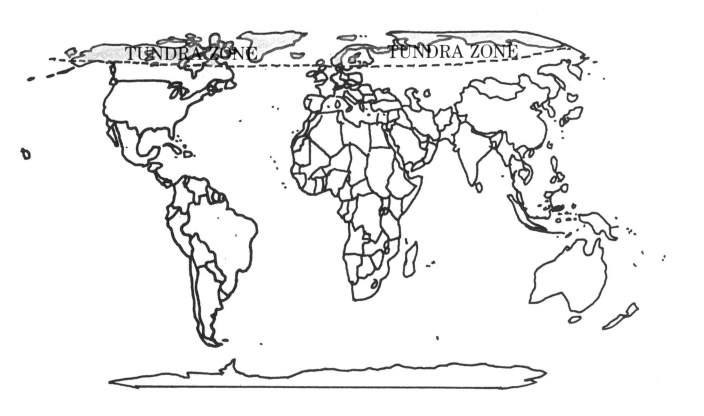

TYPHOON

A tropical *cyclone* in the China Seas

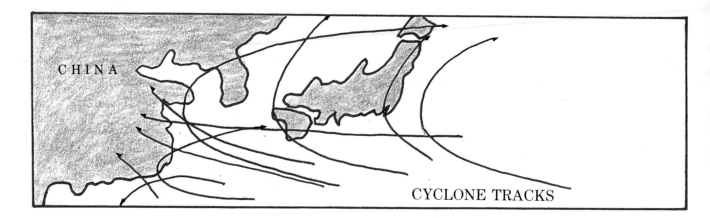

VALLEY

A long narrow depression in the *earth*'s surface, usually with
a fairly regular downward slope

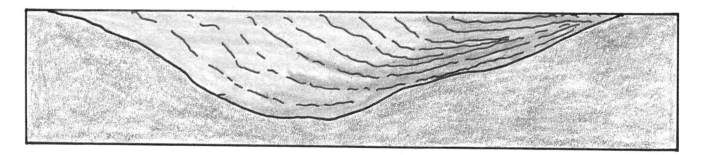

VOLCANO

A vent in the *earth*'s crust caused by magma forcing its way to
the surface (magma is molten matter)

WATERFALL

A steep descent of water from a height

IMPORTANT WATERFALLS BY CONTINENT:

Continent	Name of Waterfall	Height in Feet
Africa	Tugela (So. Africa)	2,014
Asia	Jog (India)	830
Australia	Wallaman	1,137
Europe	Mardals fossen (Norway)	2,149
North America	Yosemite (U.S.A.)	2,425
South America	Angel (Venezuela)	3,212

WATER TABLE

The surface of the ground water

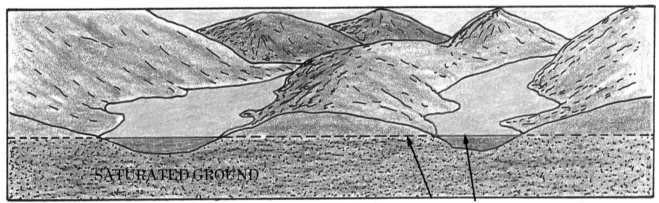

SATURATED GROUND

WATER TABLE

WINDWARD

The side upon which the *wind* blows

WIND

WINDWARD

WINDS

Currents of air moving with any speed in any direction . . . . there
are many local names for winds occurring in various places in
the world and several of them are listed in this chart:

NAME OF WIND	REGION	CHARACTERISTICS
1. BARAT	CELEBES SEA	SQUALLY, OCCASIONALLY VIOLENT
2. BARBER	U.S.A., CANADA	STRONG, CARRIES PRECIPITATION THAT FREEZES ON CONTACT WITH OBJECTS
3. BELOT	SAUDI ARABIA	STRONG, SAND CARRYING
4. BERG WIND	SOUTH AFRICA	WARM, DRY
5. BISE	FRANCE, SWITZERLAND	COLD, DRY
6. BLIZZARD	U.S.A., CANADA	WILD, PIERCING, CARRIES POWDER SNOW
7. BOHOROK	SUMATRA, INDONESIA	WARM, DRY
8. BRICKFIELDER	SOUTHERN AUSTRALIA	HOT, DRY, DUST LADEN
9. BURAN	SIBERIA, CENTRAL ASIA	COLD, FIERCE
10. BURGA	ALASKA	STRONG
11. CACIMBO	ANGOLA	REFRESHING
12. CHERGUI	MOROCCO	HOT
13. CHILE	TUNIS, NORTH AFRICA	HOT, DRY
14. CHUBASCO	MEXICO, CENTRAL AM.	VIOLENT
15. CORONAZO	MEXICO	STRONG
16. ELEPHANTA	INDIA	STRONG
17. ETESIAN	EASTERN MEDITERRANEAN	COOL
18. FOHN	ALPS	WARM, DRY
19. GHARBI	ADRIATIC & AEGEAN SEAS	WARM, MOIST
20. GIBLI	LIBYA, NO. AFRICA	HOT, DRY
21. GREGALE	SOUTH CENTRAL MEDITERRANEAN	DRY, STRONG
22. HABOOB	NORTH AFRICA	STRONG, DUSTY
23. HARMATTAN	WEST AFRICA	VERY HOT, DRY, DUSTY
24. HELM WIND	NORTHERN ENGLAND	STRONG, COLD
25. IMBAT	NORTH AFRICA	REFRESHING
26. KARABURAN	CENTRAL ASIA	STRONG, DUSTY
27. KHAMSIN	EGYPT	HOT, DRY
28. KHARIF	SOUTHERN ARABIA	STRONG, SAND LADEN
29. KOEMBANG	JAVA, INDONESIA	WARM, DRY
30. KOSHAVA	JUGOSLAVIA	STRONG, SNOW LADEN
31. LESTE	MADEIRA, AZORES	HOT, DRY
32. LEVECHE	SOUTHERN SPAIN	HOT, DRY
33. MELTEMI	EASTERN MEDITERRANEAN	STRONG, DRY
34. MISTRAL	SHORES OF NORTHWEST MEDITERRANEAN	COLD
35. NARAI	JAPAN	COLD
36. NEVADOS	HIGH VALLEYS OF ECUADOR	COLD
37. NORTHEASTER	NEW ENGLAND AND MIDDLE ATLANTIC STATES IN U.S.A.	MOIST, COLD
38. NORTHWESTER	NORTHERN U.S.A.	MODERATE TO STRONG, COOL TO COLD
39. NOR'WESTER	NEW ZEALAND	HOT, DRY
40. PAMPERO	PAMPAS OF ARGENTINA AND URUGUAY	COLD, POLAR AIR
41. PAPAGAYO	MEXICAN PLATEAU	COLD

42. PONENTE	WESTERN ITALY	REFRESHING
43. RESHABAR	CAUCASUS MTS. OF THE SOVIET UNION	STRONG
44. SANTA ANA	SOUTHERN CALIFORNIA, U.S.A.	HOT, DRY, DUSTY
45. SEISTEN	AFGHANISTAN	VIOLENT, DOWNSLOPE WIND
46. SIMOON	SAHARA AND ARABIAN DESERTS OF AFRICA	HOT, DRY
47. SIROCCO	NO. AFRICA, SICILY, SOUTHERN ITALY	HOT, DRY, DUSTY
48. SNO	SCANDINAVIA	COLD, SWIFT
49. STEPPENWIND	GERMANY	COLD
50. SUDESTADES	URUGUAY, ARGENTINA, BRAZIL	STRONG
51. SUHAILI	PERSIAN GULF	STRONG
52. SURAZOS	PERU	STRONG, COLD
53. TAKU	ALASKA	STRONG
54. TAHUANTEPECER	MEXICO	VIOLENT, COLD
55. TRAMONTANA	MEDITERRANEAN	COOL, DRY
56. ZEPHYR	WESTERN MEDITERRANEAN	SOFT, GENTLE
57. ZONDA	ARGENTINA, URUGUAY	HOT, SULTRY

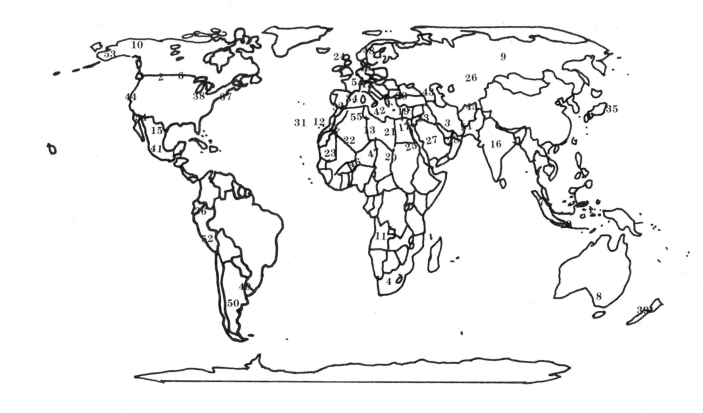